a year of Baby Afghans

BOOK 5

There's a new baby on the way—it's time to make the perfect gift! These twelve darling afghan patterns give you an entire year of soft-and-cozy blankets to crochet. In June, welcome that sweet girl or boy with an ocean of colorful fish. Treat Baby to the fun of peppermints at Christmas, or a shower of blue diamonds in April. Why not crochet a field of sunny flowers for September, or create happy "pops" of red and blue on a light throw in July? Whatever the time of year, your thoughtful gift will inspire plenty of comfort and lots of precious smiles!

LEISURE ARTS, INC.
Little Rock, Arkansas

January

January

◼◼◻◻ EASY +

Finished Size: 37" x 41" (94 cm x 104 cm)

MATERIALS

Medium Weight Yarn 🧶 **4**
[7 ounces, 364 yards
(198 grams, 333 meters) per skein]:
   White - 4 skeins
[5 ounces, 244 yards
(141 grams, 233 meters) per skein]:
   Variegated - 1 skein
Crochet hook, size J (6 mm) **or** size needed
   for gauge

GAUGE: In pattern,
            (dc, ch 1, dc) 5 times = 4³/₄"
            (12 cm);
            Rows 1-6 = 3" (7.5 cm)

Gauge Swatch: 4¹/₂"w x 3"h
                  (11.5 cm x 7.5 cm)
With White, ch 16.
Work same as Body Rows 1-6.

STITCH GUIDE

V-STITCH (*abbreviated* V-St) (uses one st or sp)
(Dc, ch 1, dc) in st or sp indicated.
POPCORN (uses one sc)
4 Dc in sc indicated, drop loop from hook, insert
hook from **front** to **back** in first dc of 4-dc group,
hook dropped loop and draw through st.

Each row is worked across length of Afghan.

BODY

With White, ch 121; place marker in third ch from hook
for Edging placement.

Row 1 (Right side)**:** Work V-St in fifth ch from hook
(**4 skipped chs count as first dc and one skipped ch**),
(skip next 2 chs, work V-St in next ch) across to last
2 chs, skip next ch, dc in last ch: 80 dc and 39 chs.

Note: Loop a short piece of yarn around any stitch to
mark Row 1 as **right** side.

Row 2: Ch 1, turn; sc in first dc, (sc, ch 2, 2 dc) in next
dc, ★ skip next ch and next dc, (sc, ch 2, 2 dc) in next dc;
repeat from ★ across to last 3 sts, skip next ch and next
dc, sc in last dc: 119 sts and 39 ch-2 sps.

Row 3: Ch 5 (**counts as first dc plus ch 2**), turn; sc in
next ch-2 sp, ★ work Popcorn in next sc, ch 3, sc in next
ch-2 sp; repeat from ★ across to last 2 sc, skip next sc,
dc in last sc: 79 sts (38 Popcorns, 39 sc, & 2 dc) and
39 ch-2 sps.

Instructions continued on page 26.

February

Finished Size: 30" x 43" (76 cm x 109 cm)

MATERIALS

Light Weight Yarn **(3)** LIGHT
[5.6 ounces, 431 yards
(160 grams, 394 meters) per skein]:
  Pink - 2 skeins
  White - 2 skeins
Crochet hook, size H (5 mm) **or** size needed
  for gauge

GAUGE: In pattern,
        16 sts and 12 rows = 4" (10 cm)

Gauge Swatch: 4" (10 cm) square
With Pink, ch 17.
Row 1: Sc in second ch from hook, dc in next ch,
(sc in next ch, dc in next ch) across: 16 sts.
Rows 2-12: Ch 1, turn; sc in first dc, dc in next sc,
(sc in next dc, dc in next sc) across.
Finish off.

BODY

With Pink, ch 103.

Row 1: Sc in second ch from hook, dc in next ch,
(sc in next ch, dc in next ch) across: 102 sts.

Row 2 (Right side)**:** Ch 1, turn; sc in first dc, dc in
next sc, (sc in next dc, dc in next sc) across.

Note: Loop a short piece of yarn around any stitch
to mark Row 2 as **right** side.

Rows 3 and 4: Repeat Row 2 twice.

Row 5: Ch 1, turn; sc in first dc, dc in next sc, (sc
in next dc, dc in next sc) 3 times changing to White
in last dc made (**Fig. 2b, page** 41), do **not** cut Pink;
working over Pink (**Fig. 2c, page** 41), sc in next dc,
dc in next sc changing to Pink, do **not** cut White;
★ (sc in next dc, dc in next sc) 6 times changing
to White in last dc made, sc in next dc, dc in next
sc changing to Pink; repeat from ★ across to last
8 sts, (sc in next dc, dc in next sc) across.

Change color in same manner throughout, working
over dropped color.

Instructions continued on page 27.

March

Finished Size: 27" (68.5 cm) square

MATERIALS

Medium Weight Yarn **[4] MEDIUM**
[7 ounces, 364 yards
(198 grams, 333 meters) per skein]:
  Off-White - 3 skeins
  Yellow - 1 skein
[3.5 ounces, 190 yards
(99 grams, 174 meters) per skein]:
  Lt Green - 1 skein
Crochet hook, size H (5 mm) **or** size needed
  for gauge
Yarn needle

GAUGE: 13 sc = 3$^{1}/_{2}$" (9 cm);
       13 rows = 3$^{1}/_{4}$" (8.25 cm);
       One Square = 5" (12.75 cm)

Gauge Swatch: 3$^{1}/_{2}$"w x 3$^{1}/_{4}$"h (9 cm x 8.25 cm)
Work same as Square through Row 13.

SQUARE (Make 25)

With Off-White, ch 14.

Row 1: Sc in second ch from hook and in each ch across: 13 sc.

Row 2 (Right side)**:** Ch 1, turn; sc in each sc across.

Note: Loop a short piece of yarn around any stitch to mark Row 2 as **right** side.

Row 3: Ch 1, turn; sc in first 6 sc changing to Lt Green in last sc made (*Fig. 2a, page* 41), do **not** cut Off-White; sc in next sc, (ch 10, sc in same st) 3 times changing to Off-White in last sc made, cut Lt Green; sc in last 6 sc: 16 sc and 3 loops.

Row 4: Ch 1, turn; sc in first 6 sc, keeping loops to **right** side, skip next sc, pull up a loop in each of next 2 sc, YO and draw through all 3 loops on hook **(counts as one sc)**, skip next sc, sc in last 6 sc: 13 sc.

Row 5: Ch 1, turn; sc in each sc across, keeping loops to **right** side.

Row 6: Ch 1, turn; sc in first 3 sc, insert hook from **front** to **back** in first loop **and** in next sc, YO and pull up a loop, YO and draw through 2 loops on hook **(sc completed)**, sc in next 5 sc, skip center loop, insert hook from **front** to **back** in last loop **and** in next sc, YO and pull up a loop, YO and draw through 2 loops on hook **(sc completed)**, sc in last 3 sc.

Instructions continued on page 28.

April

EASY

Finished Size: 34" x 45½" (86.5 cm x 115.5 cm)

MATERIALS
Medium Weight Yarn **4**
[4 ounces, 203 yards
(113 grams, 186 meters) per skein]:
   6 skeins
Crochet hook, size I (5.5 mm) **or** size needed
   for gauge

GAUGE: In pattern, 14 sts = 4" (10 cm);
         8 rows = 4⅝" (11.75 cm)

Gauge Swatch: 5½"w x 4⅝"h (14 cm x 11.75 cm)
Ch 20.
Work same as Afghan Rows 1-8.
Finish off.

STITCH GUIDE
TREBLE CROCHET (*abbreviated tr*)
YO twice, insert hook in sc indicated, YO and
pull up a loop (4 loops on hook), (YO and
draw through 2 loops on hook) 3 times.
BACK POST CLUSTER (*abbreviated BP Cluster*)
   (uses next 2 tr)
★ YO, insert hook from **back** to **front** around
post of **next** tr (*Fig. 3, page* 41), YO and pull
up a loop, YO and draw through 2 loops on
hook; repeat from ★ once **more**, YO and draw
through all 3 loops on hook.
3-DC CLUSTER (uses next 3 dc)
★ YO, insert hook in **next** dc, YO and pull
up a loop, YO and draw through 2 loops on
hook; repeat from ★ 2 times **more**, YO and
draw through all 4 loops on hook.

Each row is worked across length of Afghan.

AFGHAN
Ch 160.

Row 1: Sc in second ch from hook and in each ch
across: 159 sc.

Row 2 (Right side)**:** Ch 4 (**counts as first tr, now and
throughout**), turn; tr in next sc and in each sc across.

Note: Loop a short piece of yarn around any stitch to
mark Row 2 as **right** side.

Row 3: Ch 3 (**counts as first dc, now and
throughout**), turn; work BPdc Cluster, ★ ch 1, skip
next tr, 3 dc in next tr, ch 1, skip next tr, work BPdc
Cluster; repeat from ★ across to last tr, dc in last tr:
127 sts and 62 ch-1 sps.

Row 4: Ch 3, turn; 2 dc in next BP Cluster, ★ ch 1,
work 3-dc Cluster, ch 1, 2 dc in next BPdc Cluster;
repeat from ★ across to last dc, dc in last dc: 97 sts
and 62 ch-1 sps.

Row 5: Ch 1, turn; sc in each st and in each ch-1 sp
across: 159 sc.

Row 6: Ch 4, turn; tr in next sc and in each sc across.

Rows 7-58: Repeat Rows 3-6, 13 times.

Row 59: Ch 1, turn; sc in each tr across; finish off.

Holding 6 strands of yarn together, each 16"
(40.5 cm) long, add fringe evenly spaced across short
edges of Afghan (*Figs. 6a & b, page* 42).

May

Finished Size: 33" x 43" (84 cm x 109 cm)

MATERIALS

Light Weight Yarn **3**
[3.5 ounces, 359 yards
(100 grams, 328 meters) per skein]:
  White - 3 skeins
  Yellow **and** Lavender - 1 skein **each**
Crochet hook, size F (3.75 mm) **or** size
  needed for gauge

GAUGE: Each Strip = 3" (7.5 cm) wide

Gauge Swatch: 3" x 10½" (7.5 cm x 26.75 cm)
Work same as First Strip, page 29, working
5 Flowers on Foundation Center Row.

STITCH GUIDE

TREBLE CROCHET (*abbreviated tr*)
YO twice, insert hook in sc indicated, YO and
pull up a loop (4 loops on hook), (YO and draw
through 2 loops on hook) 3 times.

BEGINNING CLUSTER (uses one st)
YO, insert hook in third ch from hook, YO and pull
up a loop, YO and draw through 2 loops on hook,
YO, insert hook in **same** st, YO and pull up a loop,
YO and draw through 2 loops on hook, YO and
draw through all 3 loops on hook.

CLUSTER (uses one st)
★ YO, insert hook in **same** ch as beginning
Cluster, YO and pull up a loop, YO and draw
through 2 loops on hook; repeat from ★ 2 times
more, YO and draw through all 4 loops on hook.

FRONT POST SINGLE CROCHET
  (*abbreviated FPsc*)
Insert hook from **front** to **back** around st indicated
(**Fig. 3**, *page 41*), YO and pull up a loop, YO and
draw through both loops on hook.

Instructions continued on page 29.

Design by Tammy Kreimeyer 11

June

Finished Size: 30½" x 41" (77.5 cm x 104 cm)

MATERIALS

Medium Weight Yarn
[3.5 ounces, 170 yards
(100 grams, 156 meters) per skein]:
   Blue - 5 skeins
   Orange **and** Yellow - 2 skeins **each**
Crochet hook, size I (5.5 mm) **or** size
   needed for gauge

GAUGE: Each Strip = 4" (10 cm)

Gauge Swatch: 4" x 17" (10 cm x 43.25 cm)
With Orange, ch 46.
Work same as First Strip working 3 Fish on
Foundation Center Rnd.

STITCH GUIDE

TREBLE CROCHET (*abbreviated tr*)
YO twice, insert hook in st indicated, YO and
pull up a loop (4 loops on hook), (YO and draw
through 2 loops on hook) 3 times.
DECREASE (uses next 2 sps)
Pull up a loop in each of next 2 sps, YO and
draw through all 3 loops on hook (**counts as
one sc**).

FIRST STRIP

With Orange, ch 110.

Foundation Center Rnd (Right side)**:** Sc in second
ch from hook, hdc in next ch, dc in next ch, tr in
next 3 chs, dc in next ch, hdc in next ch, sc in next
ch, hdc in next ch, dc in next ch, tr in next ch, ch 4,
★ slip st in next 4 chs, sc in next ch, hdc in next ch,
dc in next ch, tr in next 3 chs, dc in next ch, hdc
in next ch, sc in next ch, hdc in next ch, dc in next
ch, tr in next ch, ch 4; repeat from ★ across to last
ch, slip st in last ch, ch 4; working in free loops of
beginning ch (**Fig. 1,** *page* 41), tr in next ch, dc in
next ch, hdc in next ch, sc in next ch, hdc in next
ch, dc in next ch, tr in next 3 chs, dc in next ch, hdc
in next ch, sc in next ch (**first Fish made**), † slip st
in next 4 chs, ch 4, tr in next ch, dc in next ch, hdc
in next ch, sc in next ch, hdc in next ch, dc in next
ch, tr in next 3 chs, dc in next ch, hdc in next ch, sc
in next ch (**Fish made**) †; repeat from † to † across,
sc in same st as last sc made; join with slip st to
first sc, finish off: 7 Fish.

Note: Loop a short piece of yarn around any stitch
to mark Foundation Center Rnd as **right** side.

Instructions continued on page 31.

Design by Sandy Rideout 13

July

EASY +

Finished Size: 31½" x 38½" (80 cm x 98 cm)

MATERIALS
Light Weight Yarn
[3 ounces, 237 yards
(85 grams, 217 meters) per skein]:
   White - 3 skeins
   Red **and** Blue - 2 skeins **each**
Crochet hook, size G (4 mm) **or** size
   needed for gauge
Yarn needle

GAUGE: Each Square = 7" (17.75 cm)

Gauge Swatch: 2" (5 cm)
Work same as Center Motif.

STITCH GUIDE
TREBLE CROCHET (*abbreviated tr*)
YO twice, insert hook in st indicated, YO and
pull up a loop (4 loops on hook), (YO and draw
through 2 loops on hook) 3 times.

MOTIF (Make 80 total - 40 using Red and White; 40 using Blue and White)

With Red or Blue, ch 6; join with slip st to form a
ring.

Rnd 1 (Right side)**:** Ch 3 (**counts as first dc, now
and throughout**), (2 dc, ch 3, 3 dc, ch 3, 7 dc) in
ring, ch 3; join with slip st to first dc: 13 dc and
3 ch-3 sps.

Note: Loop a short piece of yarn around any stitch
to mark Rnd 1 as **right** side.

Rnd 2: Ch 3, dc in next 2 dc, (2 dc, ch 3, 2 dc) in
next ch-3 sp, place marker around last ch-3 made
for st placement, dc in next 3 dc, (2 dc, ch 3, 2 dc)
in next ch-3 sp, 2 tr in next dc, tr in next dc, dc in
next dc, 3 hdc in next dc, dc in next dc, tr in next
dc, 2 tr in next dc, (2 dc, ch 3, 2 dc) in last ch-3 sp;
join with slip st to first dc, finish off: 29 sts and
3 ch-3 sps.

Rnd 3: With **right** side facing, join White with dc
in marked ch-3 sp (*see* Joining With Dc, *page* 40);
remove marker, (dc, ch 3, 2 dc) in same sp, dc in
next 7 dc, (2 dc, ch 3, 2 dc) in next ch-3 sp, dc in
next 4 sts, (dc, ch 1, dc) in next tr, dc in next 5 sts,
(dc, ch 1, dc) in next tr, dc in next 4 sts, (2 dc, ch 3,
2 dc) in next ch-3 sp, dc in last 7 dc; join with
slip st to first dc, finish off: 43 dc, 3 ch-3 sps, and
2 ch-1 sps.

CENTER MOTIF (Make 20)
Rnd 1 (Right side)**:** With White, ch 2, 8 sc in
second ch from hook; join with slip st to first sc.

Rnd 2: Ch 6 (**counts as first dc plus ch 3**), dc in
same st, ch 1, dc in next sc, ch 1, ★ (dc, ch 3, dc)
in next sc, ch 1, dc in next sc, ch 1; repeat from ★
2 times **more**; join with slip st to first dc, finish off:
12 dc, 8 ch-1 sps, and 4 ch-3 sps.

Instructions continued on page 32.

August

EASY

Finished Size: 32" x 43" (81.5 cm x 109 cm)

MATERIALS

Medium Weight Yarn 〔**MEDIUM 4**〕

[6 ounces, 315 yards
(170 grams, 288 meters) per skein]:
   White - 3 skeins
   Green - 2 skeins
   Purple - 1 skein
Crochet hook, size H (5 mm) **or** size needed
   for gauge

GAUGE: In pattern,
   14 sts and 12 rows = 4" (10 cm)

Gauge Swatch: 4" (10 cm)
With White, ch 16.
Work same as Body Rows 1-11: 14 sts.
Finish off.

STITCH GUIDE

TREBLE CROCHET (*abbreviated tr*)
YO twice, insert hook in st indicated, YO and
pull up a loop (4 loops on hook), (YO and draw
through 2 loops on hook) 3 times.

BODY

With White, ch 104.

Row 1 (Right side): Tr in fifth ch from hook,
working **around** tr just made, hdc in fourth skipped
ch (ch before tr) (**first 3 skipped chs count as first
dc**), ★ skip next ch, tr in next ch, working **around** tr
just made, hdc in skipped ch; repeat from ★ across
to last ch, dc in last ch: 102 sts.

Note: Loop a short piece of yarn around any stitch
to mark Row 1 as **right** side.

Row 2: Ch 1, turn; sc in each st across.

Row 3: Ch 2, turn; skip first sc, slip st in next sc,
(ch 2, skip next sc, slip st in next sc) across to last
2 sc, (ch 2, slip st in next sc) twice: 52 ch-2 sps.

Row 4: Turn; slip st in first ch-2 sp, ch 3 (**counts as
first dc, now and throughout**), ★ skip next slip st
and next ch, tr in next ch, working **around** tr just
made, hdc in skipped ch; repeat from ★ across to
last ch-2 sp, dc in last ch-2 sp; finish off: 102 sts.

Instructions continued on page 33.

September

EASY +

Finished Size: 35¹/₂" x 41¹/₂" (90 cm x 105.5 cm)

MATERIALS

Light Weight Yarn **3 LIGHT**

[3 ounces, 279 yards
(85 grams, 255 meters) per skein]:
  Off-White - 3 skeins
  Brown - one skein
[5 ounces, 459 yards
(140 grams, 420 meters) per skein]:
  Yellow - 2 skeins
Crochet hook, size F (3.75 mm) **or** size needed
  for gauge
Tapestry needle

GAUGE SWATCH: 3" (7.5 cm) square
Work same as Square.

STITCH GUIDE

TREBLE CROCHET (*abbreviated tr*)
YO twice, insert hook in sc indicated, YO and
pull up a loop (4 loops on hook), (YO and draw
through 2 loops on hook) 3 times.
CLUSTER (*uses next 2 sc*)
★ YO twice, insert hook in **next** sc, YO and pull
up a loop, (YO and draw through 2 loops on
hook) twice; repeat from ★ once **more**, YO and
draw through all 3 loops on hook.

SQUARE (Make 143)

With Brown, ch 4; join with slip st to form a ring.

Rnd 1 (Right side)**:** Ch 1, 16 sc in ring; join with
slip st to first sc, finish off.

Note: Loop a short piece of yarn around any stitch
to mark Rnd 1 as **right** side.

Rnd 2: With **right** side facing, join Yellow with
slip st in any sc; [ch 3, tr in next sc (**Beginning
Cluster made**)], ch 3, (work Cluster, ch 3) around;
skip beginning ch-3 and join with slip st to first tr,
finish off: 8 Clusters and 8 ch-3 sps.

Rnd 3: With **right** side facing, join Off-White with
dc in any ch-3 sp (*see Joining With Dc, page 40*); 2 dc
in same sp, ch 1, 3 dc in next ch-3 sp, ch 1, ★ (3 dc,
ch 3, 3 dc) in next ch-3 sp, ch 1, 3 dc in next
ch-3 sp, ch 1; repeat from ★ 2 times **more**, 3 dc
in same sp as first dc, ch 1, hdc in first dc to form
last corner ch-3; finish off leaving a long end for
sewing: 36 dc and 12 sps.

ASSEMBLY

Thread tapestry needle with long end. Working
through **inside** loops only on **both** pieces,
whipstitch Squares together forming 11 vertical
strips of 13 Squares each (**Fig. 5b, page 42**),
beginning in center ch of first corner ch-3 and
ending in center ch of next corner ch-3; then
whipstitch strips together in same manner.

Instructions continued on page 35.

October

EASY

Finished Size: 40" x 44" (101.5 cm x 112 cm)

MATERIALS

Medium Weight Yarn **LIGHT 3**
[3 ounces, 145 yards
(85 grams, 133 meters) per skein]:
  Variegated - 7 skeins
Medium Weight Yarn
[3.5 ounces, 170 yards
(100 grams, 156 meters) per skein]:
  Rust - 2 skeins
Crochet hook, size I (5.5 mm) **or** size needed
  for gauge

GAUGE: In pattern,
  (ch 3, sc) 7 times = 5¾" (14.5 cm);
  Rows 1-12 = 4¾" (12 cm)

Gauge Swatch: 6" x 4¾" (15.25 cm x 12 cm)
With Variegated, ch 26.
Work same as Body Rows 1-12: 8 sc and 8 ch-3 sps.
Finish off.

STITCH GUIDE

PUFF STITCH (*abbreviated Puff St*)
(YO, insert hook in st or sp indicated, YO and
pull up a loop) 3 times, YO and draw through
all 7 loops on hook.

CLUSTER
Ch 4, dc in fourth ch from hook.

BODY

With Variegated, ch 128.

Row 1 (Right side)**:** Sc in fifth ch from hook,
★ ch 3, skip next 2 chs, sc in next ch; repeat from ★
across: 42 sc and 42 sps.

Note: Loop a short piece of yarn around any stitch
to mark Row 1 as **right** side.

Row 2: Ch 3, turn; sc in first ch-3 sp, ch 3, work
Puff St in next ch-3 sp, ★ ch 3, sc in next ch-3 sp,
ch 3, work Puff St in next ch-sp; repeat from ★
across.

Row 3: Ch 3, turn; sc in first ch-3 sp, (ch 3, sc in
next ch-3 sp) across.

Row 4: Ch 3, turn; work Puff St in first ch-3 sp,
ch 3, sc in next ch-3 sp, ★ ch 3, work Puff St in next
ch-3 sp, ch 3, sc in next ch-3 sp; repeat from ★
across.

Row 5: Ch 3, turn; sc in first ch-3 sp, (ch 3, sc in
next ch-3 sp) across.

Row 6: Ch 3, turn; sc in first ch-3 sp, ch 3, work
Puff St in next ch-3 sp, ★ ch 3, sc in next ch-3 sp,
ch 3, work Puff St in next ch-3 sp; repeat from ★
across.

Rows 7-99: Repeat Rows 3-6, 23 times; then
repeat Row 3 once **more**.

Finish off.

Instructions continued on page 35.

November

Finished Size: 37³/₄" x 48¹/₂" (96 cm x 123 cm)

MATERIALS

LIGHT 3

Light Weight Yarn
[3 ounces, 279 yards
(85 grams, 255 meters) per skein]:
   Off-White - 4 skeins
   Red - 3 skeins
   Coral - 3 skeins
Crochet hook, size I (5.5 mm) **or** size needed
  for gauge

GAUGE: In pattern,
        3 repeats (Row 3) = 3³/₄" (9.5 cm);
        8 rows (Rows 6-13) = 3" (7.5 cm)

Gauge Swatch: 4³/₄" (12 cm) square
With Red, ch 16.
Work same as Afghan Rows 1-13.

STITCH GUIDE

CLUSTER (uses one ch-3 sp)
† YO, insert hook in sp indicated, YO and pull up a loop, YO and draw through 2 loops on hook †, YO twice, insert hook in **same** sp, YO and pull up a loop, (YO and draw through 2 loops on hook) twice, repeat from † to † once, YO and draw through all 4 loops on hook. Push Cluster to **right** side.

Each row is worked across length of Afghan. When joining yarn and finishing off, leave a 10" (25.5 cm) end to be worked into fringe.

AFGHAN

With Red, ch 157.

Row 1: Sc in second ch from hook and in next ch, (ch 2, sc in next 2 chs) across: 156 sc and 77 ch-2 sps.

Row 2 (Right side)**:** Ch 1, turn; sc in first sc, (sc, ch 3, sc) in next ch-2 sp and in each ch-2 sp across to last 2 sc, skip next sc, sc in last sc.

Note: Loop a short piece of yarn around any stitch to mark Row 2 as **right** side.

Instructions continued on page 36.

December

EASY +

Finished Size: 36" x 48" (91.5 cm x 122 cm)

MATERIALS

Light Weight Yarn LIGHT 3

[2.5 ounces, 165 yards
(70 grams, 150 meters) per skein]:
   Green - 6 skeins
   Red and White - 2 skeins each
Crochet hook, size G (4 mm) or size needed
   for gauge
Yarn needle

GAUGE SWATCH: 7³/₄" (19.75 cm) square
Work same as Square.

STITCH GUIDE

TREBLE CROCHET (*abbreviated tr*)
YO twice, insert hook in st indicated, YO and
pull up a loop (4 loops on hook), (YO and draw
through 2 loops on hook) 3 times.

DOUBLE TREBLE CROCHET
   (*abbreviated dtr*)
YO 3 times, insert hook in st indicated, YO and
pull up a loop (5 loops on hook), (YO and draw
through 2 loops on hook) 4 times.

SQUARE (Make 18)

With White, ch 3; join with slip st to form a ring.

Rnd 1 (Right side)**:** Ch 3 (**counts as first dc, now
and throughout**), 11 dc in ring; join with slip st to
first dc: 12 dc.

Note: Loop a short piece of yarn around any stitch
to mark Rnd 1 as **right** side.

Rnd 2: Ch 3, dc in same st, 2 dc in next dc and in
each dc around; join with slip st to first dc: 24 dc.

Rnd 3: Ch 4 (**counts as first tr**), tr in same st
changing to Red (**Fig. 2b, page** 41); ★ working over
unused color, 2 tr in next dc changing to White
in last tr made, working over unused color, 2 tr in
next dc changing to Red in last tr made; repeat
from ★ around to last dc, 2 tr in last dc; join with
slip st to first dc, finish off Red and cut White:
48 tr.

Rnd 4: With **right** side facing, join Green with dc in
any tr (**see Joining With Dc, page** 40); ch 3, dc in same
st, skip next 2 tr, ★ (dc, ch 3, dc) in next tr, skip
next 2 tr; repeat from ★ around; join with slip st to
first dc: 16 ch-3 sps.

Instructions continued on page 38.

January

Instructions continued from page 2.

Row 4: Ch 1, turn; sc in first dc, (sc, ch 2, 2 dc) in next sc, ★ skip next ch-2 sp and next Popcorn, (sc, ch 2, 2 dc) in next sc; repeat from ★ across to last ch-2 sp, skip last ch-2 sp, sc in last dc: 119 sts and 39 ch-2 sps.

Row 5: Ch 3 (counts as first dc, now and throughout), turn; work V-St in each ch-2 sp across to last 2 sc, skip next sc, dc in last sc; finish off: 80 dc and 39 chs.

Row 6: With **wrong** side facing, join Variegated with sc in first dc (*see Joining With Sc, page 40*); sc in next dc and in each dc and each ch across; finish off: 119 sc.

Row 7: With **right** side facing, join White with dc in first sc (*see Joining With Dc, page 40*); skip next sc, work V-St in next sc, (skip next 2 sc, work V-St in next sc) across to last 2 sc, skip next sc, dc in last sc: 80 dc and 39 chs.

Rows 8-65: Repeat Rows 2-7, 9 times; then repeat Rows 2-5 once more.

EDGING

Rnd 1: With **right** side facing, join Variegated with sc in first dc on Row 65; sc in same st and in each dc and each ch across to last dc, 3 sc in last dc; working in end of rows, 3 sc in first dc row, (sc in next sc row, 2 sc in next dc row) across; working in free loops of beginning ch (**Fig. 1, *page 41***), 3 sc in first ch, sc in each ch across to marked ch, 3 sc in marked ch; working in end of rows, 3 sc in first dc row, (sc in next sc row, 2 sc in next dc row) across, sc in same st as first sc; join with slip st to first sc, finish off: 444 sc.

Rnd 2: With **wrong** side facing, join White with dc in same st as joining; ch 1, dc in same st, skip next 2 sc, ★ (work V-St in next sc, skip next 2 sc) across to center sc of next corner 3-sc group, work (dc, ch 1, V-St) in center sc, skip next 2 sc; repeat from ★ 2 times **more**, (work V-St in next sc, skip next 2 sc) across, dc in same st as first dc, ch 1; join with slip st to first dc: 300 dc and 152 chs.

Rnd 3: Ch 4 (counts as first dc plus ch 1, now and throughout), turn; dc in same st, † skip next ch, work V-St in next dc, skip next dc, work V-St in next ch, (skip next 2 dc, work V-St in next ch) 38 times, skip next dc, work V-St in next dc, skip next ch, dc in next dc, ch 1, work V-St in same st, skip next ch, work V-St in next dc, skip next dc, work V-St in next ch, (skip next 2 dc, work V-St in next ch) 32 times, skip next dc, work V-St in next dc, skip next ch †, dc in next dc, ch 1, work V-St in same st, repeat from † to † once, dc in same st as first dc, ch 1; join with slip st to first dc: 316 dc and 160 chs.

Rnd 4: Ch 4, turn; dc in same st, † skip next ch, work V-St in next dc, skip next dc, work V-St in next ch, (skip next 2 dc, work V-St in next ch) 34 times, skip next dc, work V-St in next dc, skip next ch, dc in next dc, ch 1, work V-St in same st, skip next ch, work V-St in next dc, skip next dc, work V-St in next ch, (skip next 2 dc, work V-St in next ch) 40 times, skip next dc, work V-St in next dc, skip next ch †, dc in next dc, ch 1, work V-St in same st, repeat from † to † once, dc in same st as first dc, ch 1; join with slip st to first dc: 332 dc and 168 chs.

Rnd 5: Ch 3, turn; 6 dc in same st, † skip next ch-1 sp, sc in next ch-1 sp, (5 dc in next ch-1 sp, sc in next ch-1 sp) 21 times, skip next ch-1 sp, 7 dc in next dc, skip next ch-1 sp, sc in next ch-1 sp, (5 dc in next ch-1 sp, sc in next ch-1 sp) 18 times, skip next ch-1 sp †, 7 dc in next dc, repeat from † to † once; join with slip st to first dc, finish off.

● ● ● ● ● ● ● ● ● ● ● ● ● ● ● ● ●

February

Instructions continued from page 4.

Row 6: Ch 1, turn; sc in first dc, dc in next sc, (sc in next dc, dc in next sc) 3 times, with White, sc in next dc, dc in next sc, ★ with Pink, (sc in next dc, dc in next sc) 6 times, with White, sc in next dc, dc in next sc; repeat from ★ across to last 8 sts, with Pink, (sc in next dc, dc in next sc) across.

Rows 7-116: Follow Chart; at end of Row 112, cut White; at end of Row 116, do **not** finish off.

EDGING

Rnd 1 (Right side): Ch 1, with **right** side facing, work 155 sc evenly spaced across end of rows; working in free loops of beginning ch (**Fig. 1**, *page* 41), 3 sc in first ch, skip next ch, sc in next 99 chs, 3 sc in last ch; work 155 sc evenly spaced across end of rows; working in sts across Row 116, 3 sc in first sc, skip next st, sc in next 99 sts, 3 sc in last dc; join with slip st to first sc, finish off: 520 sc.

Rnd 2: With **right** side facing, join White with slip st in center sc of last corner 3-sc group made; ch 2 (**counts as first hdc, now and throughout**), hdc in same st, ch 1, skip next sc, ★ (hdc in next 3 sc, ch 1, skip next sc) across to next corner sc, 3 hdc in corner sc, ch 1, skip next sc; repeat from ★ 2 times **more**, (hdc in next 3 sc, ch 1, skip next sc) across, hdc in same st as first hdc, join with slip st to first hdc: 396 hdc and 132 ch-1 sps.

CHART

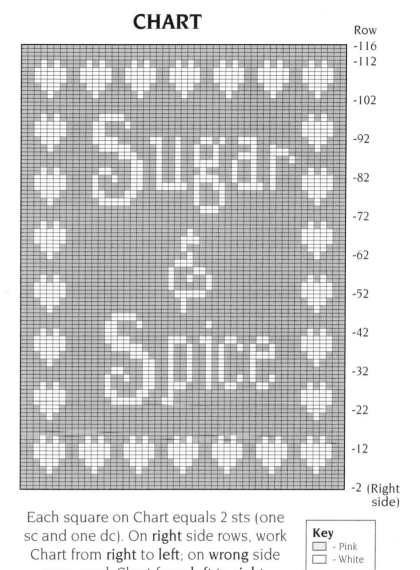

Row
-116
-112
-102
-92
-82
-72
-62
-52
-42
-32
-22
-12
-2 (Right side)

Each square on Chart equals 2 sts (one sc and one dc). On **right** side rows, work Chart from **right** to **left**; on **wrong** side rows, work Chart from **left** to **right**.

Key
▨ - Pink
☐ - White

Rnd 3: Ch 3 (counts as first dc), dc in same st, ★ † 3 dc in next ch-1 sp, skip next hdc, (dc in next 2 hdc, 3 dc in next ch-1 sp, skip next hdc) across to next corner hdc †, 3 dc in corner hdc; repeat from ★ 2 times **more**, then repeat from † to † once, dc in same st as first dc; join with slip st to first dc: 664 dc.

Rnd 4: Ch 4 (counts as first dc plus ch 1, now and throughout), 2 dc in same st, ★ † skip next dc, sc in sp **before** next dc (**Fig. 4**, *page* 41), skip next dc, (2 dc, ch 1, 2 dc) in next dc, [skip next 2 dc, sc in sp **before** next dc, skip next 2 dc, (2 dc, ch 1, 2 dc) in next dc] across to within 2 dc of next corner dc, skip next dc, sc in sp **before** next dc, skip next dc †, 2 dc in corner dc, (ch 1, 2 dc in same st) twice; repeat from ★ 2 times **more**, then repeat from † to † once, (2 dc, ch 1, dc) in same st as first dc; join with slip st to first dc: 552 dc, 136 sc, and 140 ch-1 sps.

Instructions continued on page 28.

Rnd 5: Slip st in next ch-1 sp, ch 4, (2 dc, ch 1, 2 dc) in same sp, ★ 2 dc in next ch-1 sp, (ch 1, 2 dc in same sp) twice; repeat from ★ around, dc in same sp as first dc; join with slip st to first dc: 840 dc and 280 ch-1 sps.

Rnd 6: Slip st in next ch-1 sp, ch 2, hdc in same sp, dc in next ch-1 sp, ch 2, working **around** previous dc, dc in same sp as last 2 hdc made, 2 hdc in same sp as dc just worked around, † 2 hdc in next ch-1 sp, dc in next ch-1 sp, ch 2, working **around** previous dc, dc in same sp as last 2 hdc made, 2 hdc in same sp as dc just worked around †, repeat from † to † 40 times **more**, skip next 2 dc, sc in sp **before** next dc, repeat from † to † 28 times, skip next 2 dc, sc in sp **before** next dc, repeat from † to † 42 times, skip next 2 dc, sc in sp **before** next dc, repeat from † to † 28 times, skip next 2 dc, sc in sp **before** next dc; join with slip st to first hdc, finish off.

March

Instructions continued from page 6.

Row 7: Ch 1, turn; sc in each sc across.

Row 8: Ch 1, turn; sc in first 6 sc changing to Yellow in last sc made, drop Off-White; working through center loop **and** in next sc, 5 dc in sc changing to Off-White in last dc made, cut Yellow; sc in last 6 sc: 12 sc and 5 dc.

Row 9: Ch 1, turn; sc in first 6 sc, ch 1, skip next 5 dc, sc in last 6 sc: 12 sc and one ch-1 sp.

Row 10: Ch 1, turn; sc in first 6 sc and in next ch-1 sp, sc in last 6 sc: 13 sc.

Rows 11-13: Ch 1, turn; sc in each sc across.

Do **not** finish off.

BORDER

Rnd 1 (Right side): Ch 1, turn; 2 sc in first sc, sc in next 11 sc, 3 sc in last sc; work 11 sc evenly spaced across end of rows to next corner; working in free loops of beginning ch (**Fig. 1, page** 41), 3 sc in ch at base of first sc, sc in next 11 sc, 3 sc in last ch; work 11 sc evenly spaced across end of rows to next corner, sc in same st as first sc; join with slip st to first sc, finish off: 56 sc.

Rnd 2: With **right** side facing, join Lt Green with sc in same st as joining (*see Joining With Sc, page* 40); sc in same st and in next 13 sc, ★ 3 sc in next sc, sc in next 13 sc; repeat from ★ 2 times **more**, sc in same st as first sc; join with slip st to first sc, finish off: 64 sc.

Rnd 3: With **right** side facing, join Yellow with sc in same st as joining; sc in same st and in next 15 sc, ★ 3 sc in next sc, sc in next 15 sc; repeat from ★ 2 times **more**, sc in same st as first sc; join with slip st to first sc, finish off leaving a long end for sewing: 72 sc.

ASSEMBLY

Thread yarn needle with long end. Working through **both** loops on **both** pieces, whipstitch Squares together forming 5 vertical strips of 5 Squares each (**Fig. 5a, page** 42), beginning in center sc of first corner 3-sc group and ending in center sc of next corner 3-sc group. With Yellow, whipstitch strips together in same manner.

EDGING

Rnd 1: With **right** side facing, join Off-White with sc in any corner sc; sc in same st and in next 17 sc, ★ † (sc in next joining and in next 17 sc) across to next corner sc †, 3 sc in corner sc, sc in next 17 sc; repeat from ★ 2 times **more**, then repeat from † to † once, sc in same st as first sc; join with slip st to first sc: 368 sc.

Rnd 2: Ch 7 (counts as first dc **plus ch 4**), dc in fourth ch from hook and in same st as joining, skip next 3 sc, ★ (dc, ch 4, dc in fourth ch from hook, dc) in next sc, skip next 3 sc; repeat from ★ around; join with slip st to first dc, finish off.

May

Instructions continued from page 10.

FIRST STRIP

Foundation Center Row (Right side)**:** With Yellow, ch 3, work beginning Cluster, ch 3, (work Cluster, ch 3) 5 times; join with slip st to top of beginning Cluster (**first Flower made**), ★ ch 9, work beginning Cluster, ch 3, (work Cluster, ch 3) twice, skip next 2 chs on ch-9 from last Cluster made, insert hook in next ch, YO and pull up a loop, insert hook in same ch as beginning Cluster, YO and pull up a loop, YO and draw through 2 loops on hook, (YO, insert hook in same ch as beginning Cluster, YO and pull up a loop, YO and draw through 2 loops on hook) twice, YO and draw through all 4 loops on hook, ch 3, (work Cluster, ch 3) twice; join with slip st to top of beginning Cluster (**Flower made**); repeat from ★ 19 times **more**; finish off: 21 Flowers.

Note: Loop a short piece of yarn around first Flower to mark Foundation Center Row as **right** side **and** bottom.

Rnd 1: With **right** side facing, join White with sc in third ch-3 sp after beginning Cluster on first Flower (*see Joining With Sc, page* 40); sc in same sp, work FPsc around next Cluster, † (2 sc in next ch-3 sp, work FPsc around next Cluster) twice, sc in next ch-3 sp, insert hook in same sp, YO and pull up a loop, insert hook in next ch, YO and pull up a loop, YO and draw through all 3 loops on hook, sc in next ch, insert hook in next ch, YO and pull up a loop, insert hook from **front** to **back** around next Cluster, YO and pull up a loop, YO and draw through all 3 loops on hook †; repeat from † to † across to last Flower, (2 sc in next ch-3 sp, work FPsc around next Cluster) 5 times; working along opposite side of Foundation Center Row and in free loops of ch between Flowers (**Fig. 1, page** 41), sc in next ch-3 sp, insert hook in same sp, YO and pull up a loop, insert hook in next ch, YO and pull up a loop, YO and draw through all 3 loops on hook, sc in next ch, insert hook in next ch, YO and pull up a loop, insert hook from **front** to **back** around next Cluster, YO and pull up a loop, YO and draw through all 3 loops on hook, repeat from † to † across to last 2 ch-3 sps, (2 sc in next ch-3 sp, work FPsc around next Cluster) twice; join with slip st to first sc: 418 sts.

Instructions continued on page 30.

Rnd 2: Ch 3 (counts as first dc, now and throughout), dc in same st, ch 3, 2 dc in next sc, [skip next FPsc, (ch 3, 2 dc in next sc) twice] 2 times, † skip next 5 sts, tr in next sc, ch 3, working **behind** last tr made, tr in third skipped st, ★ skip next 2 sts, 2 dc in next sc, ch 3, 2 dc in next sc, skip next 5 sts, tr in next sc, ch 3, working **behind** last tr made, tr in third skipped st; repeat from ★ 18 times **more** †, skip next 2 sts, 2 dc in next sc, ch 3, 2 dc in next sc, [skip next FPsc, (ch 3, 2 dc in next sc) twice] 3 times, repeat from † to † once, skip next 2 sts, (2 dc in next sc, ch 3) twice, skip last FPsc; join with slip st to first dc, finish off: 92 ch-3 sps.

The method used to connect the Strips is a no-sew joining also known as "join-as-you-go". After the First Strip is made, each remaining Strip is worked to the last round, then crocheted together as the last round is worked. Holding Strips with **wrong** sides together, slip stitch in space as indicated.

SECOND STRIP

With Purple, work same as First Strip through Rnd 1: 418 sts.

Rnd 2 (Joining Rnd)**:** Ch 3, dc in same st, ch 3, 2 dc in next sc, [skip next FPsc, (ch 3, 2 dc in next sc) twice] 2 times, skip next 5 sts, tr in next sc, ch 3, working **behind** last tr made, tr in third skipped st, ★ skip next 2 sts, 2 dc in next sc, ch 3, 2 dc in next sc, skip next 5 sts, tr in next sc, ch 3, working **behind** last tr made, tr in third skipped st; repeat from ★ 18 times **more**, skip next 2 sts, [(2 dc in next sc, ch 3) twice, skip next FPsc] 3 times, 2 dc in next sc, ch 1, with **right** side facing, slip st in corresponding ch-3 sp on **previous Strip**, ch 1, 2 dc in next sc on **new Strip**, † skip next 5 sts, tr in next sc, ch 1, slip st in next ch-3 on **previous Strip**, ch 1, working **behind** last tr made on **new Strip**, tr in third skipped st, skip next 2 sts, 2 dc in next sc, ch 1, slip st next ch-3 sp on **previous Strip**, ch 1, 2 dc in next sc on **new Strip** †; repeat from † to † 19 times **more**, ch 3, skip last FPsc; join with slip st to first dc, finish off.

THIRD STRIP

Work same as First Strip through Rnd 1: 418 sts.

Rnd 2 (Joining Rnd)**:** Ch 3, dc in same st, ch 3, 2 dc in next sc, [skip next FPsc, (ch 3, 2 dc in next sc) twice] 2 times, skip next 5 sts, tr in next sc, ch 3, working **behind** last tr made, tr in third skipped st, ★ skip next 2 sts, 2 dc in next sc, ch 3, 2 dc in next sc, skip next 5 sts, tr in next sc, ch 3, working **behind** last tr made, tr in third skipped st; repeat from ★ 18 times **more**, skip next 2 sts, [(2 dc in next sc, ch 3) twice, skip next FPsc] 3 times, 2 dc in next sc, ch 1, slip st in corresponding ch-3 sp on **previous Strip**, ch 1, with **right** side facing, 2 dc in next sc on **new Strip**, † skip next 5 sts, tr in next sc, ch 1, slip st in next ch-3 on **previous Strip**, ch 1, working **behind** last tr made on **new Strip**, tr in third skipped st, skip next 2 sts, 2 dc in next sc, ch 1, slip st next ch-3 sp on **previous Strip**, ch 1, 2 dc in next sc on **new Strip** †; repeat from † to † 19 times **more**, ch 3, skip last FPsc; join with slip st to first dc, finish off.

REMAINING 8 STRIPS

Repeat Second Strip and Third Strip 4 times.

June

Instructions continued from page 12.

Rnd 1: With **right** side facing, join Blue with slip st in center sc of 3-sc group on Fish nose; ch 4 **(counts as first tr)**, 8 tr in same st, 2 tr in next sc, dc in next hdc, hdc in next dc, sc in next 3 tr, hdc in next dc, dc in next hdc, tr in next sc, dc in next hdc, hdc in next dc, sc in next tr and in next ch, ★ skip next slip st, working around slip sts and in chs, tr in next 3 chs and in next sc, dc in next hdc, hdc in next dc, sc in next 3 tr, hdc in next dc, dc in next hdc, tr in next sc, dc in next hdc, hdc in next dc, sc in next tr and in next ch; repeat from ★ across, 9 tr in same ch as last slip st on Foundation Rnd, skip next 3 chs, sc in next ch and in next tr, hdc in next dc, dc in next hdc, tr in next sc, dc in next hdc, hdc in next dc, sc in next 3 tr, hdc in next dc, dc in next hdc, † tr in next sc, working around slip sts and in chs, tr in next 3 chs, skip next 3 chs, sc in next ch and in next tr, hdc in next dc, dc in next hdc, tr in next sc, dc in next hdc, hdc in next dc, sc in next 3 tr, hdc in next dc, dc in next hdc †; repeat from † to † across to last sc, 2 tr in last sc; join with slip st to first tr: 238 sts.

Rnd 2: Ch 3 **(counts as first dc, now and throughout)**, dc in same st, 2 dc in each of next 3 tr, 3 dc in next tr, 2 dc in each of next 4 tr, dc in next 110 sts, 2 dc in each of next 4 tr, 3 dc in next tr, 2 dc in each of next 4 tr, dc in next st and in each st across; join with slip st to first dc: 258 dc.

Rnd 3: Ch 1, sc in same st, (ch 3, skip next dc, sc in next dc) 9 times, (ch 3, skip next 2 dc, sc in next dc) 37 times, (ch 3, skip next dc, sc in next dc) 9 times, ch 3, skip next 2 dc, (sc in next dc, ch 3, skip next 2 dc) across; join with slip st to first sc, finish off: 92 ch-3 sps.

The method used to connect the Strips is a no-sew joining also known as "join-as-you-go". After the First Strip is made, each remaining Strip is worked to the last round, then crocheted together as the last round is worked. Holding Strips with right sides together, sc in space as indicated.

SECOND STRIP

Beginning with Yellow, work same as First Strip through Rnd 2: 258 dc.

Rnd 3 (Joining Rnd): Ch 1, sc in same st, (ch 3, skip next dc, sc in next dc) 9 times, ch 1, with **right** sides facing and having Strip in opposite direction than the previous Strip, sc in corresponding ch-3 sp on **previous Strip**, ch 1, skip next 2 dc on **new Strip**, sc in next dc, ★ ch 1, sc in next ch-3 sp on **previous Strip**, ch 1, skip next 2 dc on **new Strip**, sc in next dc; repeat from ★ 35 times **more**, (ch 3, skip next dc, sc in next dc) 9 times, ch 3, skip next 2 dc, (sc in next dc, ch 3, skip next 2 dc) across; join with slip st to first sc, finish off.

THIRD STRIP

Work same as First Strip through Rnd 2: 258 dc.

Rnd 3 (Joining Rnd): Ch 1, sc in same st, (ch 3, skip next dc, sc in next dc) 9 times, (ch 3, skip next 2 dc, sc in next dc) 37 times, (ch 3, skip next dc, sc in next dc) 9 times, ch 1, with **right** sides facing and having Strip in opposite direction than the previous Strip, sc in corresponding ch-3 sp on **previous Strip**, ch 1, skip next 2 dc on **new Strip**, ★ sc in next dc, ch 1, sc in next ch-3 sp on **previous Strip**, ch 1, skip next 2 dc on **new Strip**; repeat from ★ across; join with slip st to first sc, finish off.

Instructions continued on page 32.

REMAINING 4 STRIPS

Repeat Second Strip and Third Strip twice.

EDGING

Rnd 1: With **right** side facing, join Yellow with sc in joining sc between first 2 Strips at top right edge (*see Joining With Sc, page* 40); † ch 3, [(sc in next ch-3 sp, ch 3) 9 times, sc in joining sc, ch 3] 5 times, (sc in next ch-3 sp, ch 3) around to next joining sc †, sc in joining sc, repeat from † to † once; join with slip st to first sc, finish off.

Rnd 2: With **right** side facing, join Orange with sc in second ch-3 sp from joining slip st; ch 3, (sc in next ch-3 sp, ch 3) 7 times, decrease, † ch 3, (sc in next ch-3 sp, ch 3) 8 times, decrease †; repeat from † to † 3 times **more**, ch 3, (sc in next ch-3 sp, ch 3) around to last ch-3 sp on same Strip, decrease, repeat from † to † 5 times, ch 3, (sc in next ch-3 sp, ch 3) around to last 2 ch-3 sps, decrease, ch 3; join with slip st to first sc, finish off.

Rnd 3: With Yellow, repeat Rnd 2.

Rnd 4: Repeat Rnd 2.

July

Instructions continued from page 14.

ASSEMBLY
SQUARE

Using Square Diagram as a guide and White, working in **both** loops of **both** pieces (**Fig. 5a**, *page* 42), whipstitch 4 Motifs and one Center Motif together to form the Square.

Repeat for remaining Motifs and Center Motifs to make a total of 20 Squares.

AFGHAN

Using Afghan Diagram as a guide on page 33 and White, working in **both** loops of **both** pieces, whipstitch Squares together forming 4 vertical strips of 5 Squares each.

EDGING

Rnd 1: With **right** side facing, join White with dc in ch-3 sp at top right corner (point A on Afghan Diagram); (dc, ch 3, 2 dc) in same sp, ★ † dc in next 11 dc, [dc in next ch, dc in next 2 chs (same as seam), dc in next ch, dc in next 11 dc] across to next corner ch-3 sp †, (2 dc, ch 3, 2 dc) in corner ch-3 sp; repeat from ★ 2 times **more**, then repeat from † to † once; join with slip st to first dc, finish off: 540 dc and 4 ch-3 sps.

Rnds 2 and 3: With **right** side facing, join Red with dc in top right corner ch-3 sp, dc in same sp; † dc in next dc and in each dc across to next corner ch-3 sp, 2 dc in corner ch-3 sp changing to Blue in last dc made (**Fig. 2c**, *page* 41), cut Red, ch 3, 2 dc in same sp, dc in next dc and in each dc across to next corner ch-3 sp †, 2 dc in corner ch-3 sp changing to Red in last dc made, cut Blue, ch 3, 2 dc in same sp, repeat from † to † once, 2 dc in same sp as first dc, ch 3; join with slip st to first dc, finish off: 572 dc and 4 ch-3 sps.

SQUARE DIAGRAM

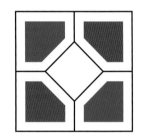

Rnd 4: With **right** side facing, join White with sc in any corner ch-3 sp *(see Joining With Sc, page 40)*; ch 1, sc in same sp, ch 1, ★ (skip next dc, sc in next dc, ch 1) across to next corner ch-3 sp, (sc, ch 1) twice in corner ch-3 sp; repeat from ★ 2 times **more**, (skip next dc, sc in next dc, ch 1) across; join with slip st to first sc.

Rnd 5: Ch 1, (slip st in next ch-1 sp, ch 2) around; join with slip st to first slip st, finish off.

AFGHAN DIAGRAM

● Point A

August

Instructions continued from page 16.

Row 5: With **right** side facing, join Green with sc in first dc *(see Joining With Sc, page 40)*; sc in next st and in each st across.

Row 6: Ch 2, turn; skip first sc, slip st in next sc, (ch 2, skip next sc, slip st in next sc) across to last 2 sc, (ch 2, slip st in next sc) twice; finish off: 52 ch-2 sps.

Row 7: With **right** side facing, join Purple with dc in first ch-2 sp *(see Joining With Dc, page 40)*; ★ skip next slip st and next ch, tr in next ch, working **around** tr just made, hdc in skipped ch; repeat from ★ across to last ch-2 sp, dc in last ch-2 sp; finish off: 102 sts.

Row 8: With **wrong** side facing, join Green with sc in first dc; sc in next st and in each st across.

Row 9: Ch 2, turn; skip first sc, slip st in next sc, (ch 2, skip next sc, slip st in next sc) across to last 2 sc, (ch 2, slip st in next sc) twice; finish off: 52 ch-2 sps.

Row 10: With **wrong** side facing, join White with dc in first ch-2 sp; ★ skip next slip st and next ch, tr in next ch, working **around** tr just made, hdc in skipped ch; repeat from ★ across to last ch-2 sp, dc in last ch-2 sp: 102 sts.

Instructions continued on page 34.

Row 11: Ch 1, turn; sc in each st across.

Row 12: Ch 2, turn; skip first sc, slip st in next sc, (ch 2, skip next sc, slip st in next sc) across to last 2 sc, (ch 2, slip st in next sc) twice: 52 ch-2 sps.

Row 13: Turn; slip st in first ch-2 sp, ch 3, ★ skip next slip st and next ch, tr in next ch, working **around** tr just made, hdc in skipped ch; repeat from ★ across to last ch-2 sp, dc in last ch-2 sp; finish off: 102 sts.

Row 14: With **wrong** side facing, join Green with sc in first dc; sc in next st and in each st across.

Row 15: Ch 2, turn; skip first sc, slip st in next sc, (ch 2, skip next sc, slip st in next sc) across to last 2 sc, (ch 2, slip st in next sc) twice; finish off: 52 ch-2 sps.

Row 16: With **wrong** side facing, join Purple with dc in first ch-2 sp; ★ skip next slip st and next ch, tr in next ch, working **around** tr just made, hdc in skipped ch; repeat from ★ across to last ch-2 sp, dc in last ch-2 sp; finish off: 102 sts.

Row 17: With **right** side facing, join Green with sc in first dc; sc in next st and in each st across.

Row 18: Ch 2, turn; skip first sc, slip st in next sc, (ch 2, skip next sc, slip st in next sc) across to last 2 sc, (ch 2, slip st in next sc) twice; finish off: 52 ch-2 sps.

Row 19: With **right** side facing, join White with dc in first ch-2 sp; ★ skip next slip st and next ch, tr in next ch, working **around** tr just made, hdc in skipped ch; repeat from ★ across to last ch-2 sp, dc in last ch-2 sp; finish off: 102 sts.

Rows 20-22: Repeat Rows 11-13.

Rows 23-120: Repeat Rows 5-22, 5 times; then repeat Rows 5-12 once **more**.

Row 121: Turn; slip st in first ch-2 sp, ch 3, ★ skip next slip st and next ch, tr in next ch, working **around** tr just made, hdc in skipped ch; repeat from ★ across to last ch-2 sp, dc in last ch-2 sp; do **not** finish off: 102 sts.

EDGING

Rnd 1: Ch 3, do **not** turn; working in end of rows, skip first 2 rows, (slip st in next row, ch 3) twice, [skip next row, (slip st in next row, ch 3) twice] across to last 3 rows, skip next row, slip st in next row, ch 3, skip last row; working in free loops of beginning ch (**Fig. 1,** *page 41*), (slip st, ch 3) twice in first ch, (skip next ch, slip st in next ch, ch 3) across to last 3 chs, skip next 2 chs, (slip st, ch 3) twice in last ch; working in end of rows, skip first row, ch 3, slip st in next row, [skip next row, (slip st in next row, ch 3) twice] across to last 2 rows, skip last 2 rows; working across Row 121, (slip st, ch 3) twice in first dc, skip next st, (slip st in next st, ch 3, skip next st) across to last dc, slip st in last dc, ch 3; join with slip st to base of first slip st, finish off.

Rnd 2: With **right** side facing, join Green with slip st in any corner ch-3 sp; ch 3, slip st in same sp, ch 3, ★ (slip st in next ch-3 sp, ch 3) across to next corner ch-3 sp, (slip st, ch 3) twice in next corner ch-3 sp; repeat from ★ 2 times **more**, (slip st in next ch-3 sp, ch 3) across; join with slip st to first slip st, finish off.

Rnd 3: With White, repeat Rnd 2.

Rnd 4: With Purple, repeat Rnd 2.

Rnd 5: With White, Repeat Rnd 2.

● ● ● ● ● ● ● ● ● ●

September

Instructions continued from page 18.

EDGING

Rnd 1: With **right** side facing, join Yellow with sc in any corner ch-3 sp (*see Joining With Sc, page* 40); ch 3, sc in same sp, ch 3, ★ (sc in next sp, ch 3) across to next corner ch-3 sp, (sc, ch 3) twice in corner sp; repeat from ★ 2 times **more**, (sc in next sp, ch 3) across; join with slip st to first sc: 192 ch-3 sps.

Rnd 2: Ch 1, 3 sc in next ch-3 sp and in each ch-3 sp around; join with slip st to first sc, finish off: 576 sc.

Rnd 3: With **right** side facing, join Off-White with sc in center sc of any corner 3-sc group; ch 3, skip next sc, ★ sc in next sc, ch 3, skip next sc; repeat from ★ around; join with slip st to first sc, finish off.

October

Instructions continued from page 20.

TRIM

Rnd 1: With **right** side facing, join Rust with slip st in second ch-3 sp on Row 99; ♥ work Puff St in same sp, ch 3, (sc in next ch-3 sp, ch 3) twice, work Puff St in next ch-3 sp, slip st in next sc and in next ch-3 sp ♥; repeat from ♥ to ♥ 9 times **more**, work Cluster, (slip st, ch 7, slip st) in last sc, work Cluster; working in end of rows, skip first 2 rows, † (slip st, work Puff St) in next row, ch 3, skip next row, (sc in next row, ch 3, skip next row) twice, work Puff St in next row, slip st in next row †; repeat from † to † across to last row, work Cluster, skip last row; working in sps across beginning ch and in free loops (**Fig.** 1, *page* 41), (slip st, ch 7, slip st) in first ch, work Cluster, skip first sp, (slip st, work Puff St) in next sp, ch 3, (sc in next sp, ch 3) twice, work Puff St in next sp, ★ slip st in next ch (same ch as sc) and in next sp, work Puff St in same sp, ch 3, (sc in next sp, ch 3) twice, work Puff St in next sp; repeat from ★ 8 times **more**, slip st in next ch (same ch as sc), work Cluster, (slip st, ch 7, slip st) in last sp, work Cluster; working in end of rows, skip first 2 rows, repeat from † to † across to last row, work Cluster, skip last row, (slip st, ch 7, slip st) in first ch-3 sp on Row 99, work Cluster; join with slip st to joining slip st, finish off: 132 ch-3 sps, 4 ch-7 sps, 88 Puff Sts, and 8 Clusters.

EDGE POINTS
FIRST POINT

With **wrong** side facing, join Rust with slip st in first ch-3 sp after corner; ch 3, work Puff St in same sp, ch 3, sc in next ch-3 sp, ch 3, work Puff St in next ch-3 sp, ch 1, leave remaining sts unworked, **turn**; (slip st, ch 3, work Puff St) in first ch-3 sp, work Cluster, work Puff St in last ch-3 sp; finish off.

REMAINING POINTS

With **wrong** side facing, skip next 2 Puff Sts from previous Point and join Rust with slip st in next ch-3 sp; ch 3, work Puff St in same sp, ch 3, sc in next ch-3 sp, ch 3, work Puff St in next ch-3 sp, ch 1, leave remaining sts unworked, **turn**; (slip st, ch 3, work Puff St) in first ch-3 sp, work Cluster, work Puff St in last ch-3 sp; finish off.

Instructions continued on page 36.

Repeat Edge Points around entire Afghan, for a total of 44 Points.

EDGING

Rnd 1: With **right** side facing, skip first Cluster after any corner ch-7 sp and join Rust with slip st in next slip st; slip st in next Puff St, ★ ♥ work Cluster, (slip st in next Puff St, work Cluster) twice, (slip st, work Cluster) twice in next Cluster (ch-3 sp), (slip st in next Puff St, work Cluster) twice, † slip st in next 2 slip sts (between Puff Sts), work Cluster, (slip st in next Puff St, work Cluster) twice, (slip st, work Cluster) twice in next Cluster, (slip st in next Puff St, work Cluster) twice †; repeat from † to † across to next corner, slip st in next Puff St and in next slip st, work Cluster, (slip st, work Cluster) twice in next corner ch-7 sp, skip next Cluster ♥, slip st in next slip st and in next Puff St; repeat from ★ 2 times **more**, then repeat from ♥ to ♥ once; join with slip st to joining slip st: 320 Clusters.

Rnd 2: Slip st in next Cluster, ★ ♥ † ch 3, (slip st in next Cluster, ch 3) 5 times, slip st in next 2 Clusters †; repeat from † to † across to corner Cluster, ch 5, (slip st, ch 5) twice in corner Cluster ♥, slip st in next 2 Clusters; repeat from ★ 2 times **more**, then repeat from ♥ to ♥ once, slip st in last Cluster; join with slip st to joining slip st, finish off.

November

Instructions continued from page 22.

Row 3: Ch 3 **(counts as first dc, now and throughout)**, turn; (sc, ch 1, dc, ch 1, sc) in next ch-3 sp, ★ (sc, ch 1, work Cluster, ch 1, sc) in next ch-3 sp, (sc, ch 1, dc, ch 1, sc) in next ch-3 sp; repeat from ★ across to last 2 sc, skip next sc, dc in last sc: 41 dc, 38 Clusters, and 154 ch-1 sps.

Row 4: Ch 3, turn; skip next sc and next ch-1 sp, (sc, ch 3, sc) in next dc, ★ skip next 2 ch-1 sps, (sc, ch 3, sc) in next Cluster, skip next 2 ch-1 sps, (sc, ch 3, sc) in next dc; repeat from ★ across to last ch-1 sp, skip last ch-1 sp and next sc, dc in last dc: 77 ch-3 sps.

Row 5: Ch 1, turn; sc in first dc, 3 sc in next ch-3 sp and in each ch-3 sp across to last 2 sts, skip next sc, sc in last dc; finish off: 233 sc.

Row 6: With **right** side facing, join Off-White with sc in first sc (*see Joining With Sc, page 40*); skip next sc, (sc, ch 3, sc) in next sc, ★ skip next 2 sc, (sc, ch 3, sc) in next sc; repeat from ★ across to last 2 sc, skip next sc, sc in last sc: 77 ch-3 sps.

Row 7: Ch 3, turn; (sc, ch 1, work Cluster, ch 1, sc) in next ch-3 sp, ★ (sc, ch 1, dc, ch 1, sc) in next ch-3 sp, (sc, ch 1, work Cluster, ch 1, sc) in next ch-3 sp; repeat from ★ across to last 2 sc, skip next sc, dc in last sc: 40 dc, 39 Clusters, and 154 ch-1 sps.

Row 8: Ch 3, turn; skip next sc and next ch-1 sp, (sc, ch 3, sc) in next Cluster, ★ skip next 2 ch-1 sps, (sc, ch 3, sc) in next dc, skip next 2 ch-1 sps, (sc, ch 3, sc) in next Cluster; repeat from ★ across to last ch-1 sp, skip last ch-1 sp and next sc, dc in last dc; finish off: 77 ch-3 sps.

Row 9: With **wrong** side facing, join Coral with sc in first dc; 3 sc in next ch-3 sp and in each ch-3 sp across to last 2 sts, skip next sc, sc in last dc: 233 sc.

Row 10: Ch 1, turn; sc in first sc, skip next sc, (sc, ch 3, sc) in next sc, ★ skip next 2 sc, (sc, ch 3, sc) in next sc; repeat from ★ across to last 2 sc, skip next sc, sc in last sc: 77 ch-3 sps.

Row 11: Ch 3, turn; (sc, ch 1, dc, ch 1, sc) in next ch-3 sp, ★ (sc, ch 1, work Cluster, ch 1, sc) in next ch-3 sp, (sc, ch 1, dc, ch 1, sc) in next ch-3 sp; repeat from ★ across to last 2 sc, skip next sc, dc in last sc: 41 dc, 38 Clusters, and 154 ch-1 sps.

Row 12: Ch 3, turn; skip next sc and next ch-1 sp, (sc, ch 3, sc) in next dc, ★ skip next 2 ch-1 sps, (sc, ch 3, sc) in next Cluster, skip next 2 ch-1 sps, (sc, ch 3, sc) in next dc; repeat from ★ across to last ch-1 sp, skip last ch-1 sp and next sc, dc in last dc: 77 ch-3 sps.

Row 13: Ch 1, turn; sc in first dc, 3 sc in next ch-3 sp and in each ch-3 sp across to last 2 sts, skip next sc, sc in last dc; finish off: 233 sc.

Row 14: With **right** side facing, join Off-White with sc in first sc; skip next sc, (sc, ch 3, sc) in next sc, ★ skip next 2 sc, (sc, ch 3, sc) in next sc; repeat from ★ across to last 2 sc, skip next sc, sc in last sc: 77 ch-3 sps.

Row 15: Ch 3, turn; (sc, ch 1, work Cluster, ch 1, sc) in next ch-3 sp, ★ (sc, ch 1, dc, ch 1, sc) in next ch-3 sp, (sc, ch 1, work Cluster, ch 1, sc) in next ch-3 sp; repeat from ★ across to last 2 sc, skip next sc, dc in last sc: 40 dc, 39 Clusters, and 154 ch-1 sps.

Row 16: Ch 3, turn; skip next sc and next ch-1 sp, (sc, ch 3, sc) in next Cluster, ★ skip next 2 ch-1 sps, (sc, ch 3, sc) in next dc, skip next 2 ch-1 sps, (sc, ch 3, sc) in next Cluster; repeat from ★ across to last ch-1 sp, skip last ch-1 sp and next sc, dc in last dc; finish off: 77 ch-3 sps.

Row 17: With **wrong** side facing, join Red with sc in first dc; 3 sc in next ch-3 sp and in each ch-3 sp across to last 2 sts, skip next sc, sc in last dc: 233 sc.

Row 18: Ch 1, turn; sc in first sc, skip next sc, (sc, ch 3, sc) in next sc, ★ skip next 2 sc, (sc, ch 3, sc) in next sc; repeat from ★ across to last 2 sc, skip next sc, sc in last sc: 77 ch-3 sps.

Row 19: Ch 3, turn; (sc, ch 1, dc, ch 1, sc) in next ch-3 sp, ★ (sc, ch 1, work Cluster, ch 1, sc) in next ch-3 sp, (sc, ch 1, dc, ch 1, sc) in next ch-3 sp; repeat from ★ across to last 2 sc, skip next sc, dc in last sc: 41 dc, 38 Clusters, and 154 ch-1 sps.

Row 20: Ch 3, turn; skip next sc and next ch-1 sp, (sc, ch 3, sc) in next dc, ★ skip next 2 ch-1 sps, (sc, ch 3, sc) in next Cluster, skip next 2 ch-1 sps, (sc, ch 3, sc) in next dc; repeat from ★ across to last ch-1 sp, skip last ch-1 sp and next sc, dc in last dc: 77 ch-3 sps.

Row 21: Ch 1, turn; sc in first dc, 3 sc in next ch-3 sp and in each ch-3 sp across to last 2 sts, skip next sc, sc in last dc; finish off: 233 sc.

Rows 22-100: Repeat Rows 6-21, 4 times; then repeat Rows 6-20 once **more**: 77 ch-3 sps.

Row 101: Ch 1, turn; sc in first dc, 2 sc in next ch-3 sp, (ch 1, 2 sc in next ch-3 sp) across to last 2 sts, skip next sc, sc in last dc; finish off.

Holding 2 strands of each color yarn together, each 16" (40.5 cm) long (**Fig. 6a & b, page 42**), add additional fringe across short edges of Afghan.

December

Instructions continued from page 24.

Rnd 5: Slip st in next ch-3 sp, ch 5 (**counts as first dtr**), (2 dtr, ch 2, 3 dtr) in same sp, ch 1, 3 tr in next ch-3 sp, ch 1, 3 dc in next ch-3 sp, ch 1, 3 tr in next ch-3 sp, ch 1, ★ (3 dtr, ch 2, 3 dtr) in next ch-3 sp, ch 1, 3 tr in next ch-3 sp, ch 1, 3 dc in next ch-3 sp, ch 1, 3 tr in next ch-3 sp, ch 1; repeat from ★ 2 times **more**; join with slip st to first dtr: 60 sts and 20 sps.

Rnd 6: Slip st in next 2 dtr and in next corner ch-2 sp, ch 4, (2 tr, ch 2, 3 tr) in same sp, ch 1, (3 tr in next ch-1 sp, ch 1) 4 times, ★ (3 tr, ch 2, 3 tr) in next corner ch-2 sp, ch 1, (3 tr in next ch-1 sp, ch 1) 4 times; repeat from ★ 2 times **more**; join with slip st to first tr: 72 tr and 24 sps.

Rnd 7: Ch 3, dc in next 2 tr, 5 dc in next corner ch-2 sp, ★ dc in next 3 tr, (dc in next ch-1 sp and in next 3 tr) 5 times, 5 dc in next corner ch-2 sp; repeat from ★ 2 times **more**, (dc in next 3 tr and in next ch-1 sp) 5 times; join with slip st to first dc: 112 dc.

With **wrong** sides together and Green, working through **both** loops, and beginning in center dc of first corner and ending in center dc of next corner (Fig. 5a, page 42), whipstitch 6 Squares together to form one strip; repeat for remaining 2 strips; do **not** join strips.

BORDERS
FIRST STRIP
Row 1: With **right** side of one Strip facing (left edge) and working in each dc and in same dc as each joining, join Red with slip st in center dc of first corner 5-dc group; ch 4, tr in next dc changing to White, tr in next 2 dc changing to Red in last tr made, ★ tr in next 2 dc changing to White in last tr made, tr in next 2 dc changing to Red in last tr made; repeat from ★ across to within one dc of center dc of next corner 5-dc group, tr in next 2 dc; finish off Red and cut White: 174 tr.

Row 2: With **wrong** side facing, join Green with dc in first tr; skip next tr, (dc, ch 3, dc) in next tr, ★ skip next 3 tr, (dc, ch 3, dc) in next tr; repeat from ★ across to last 3 tr, skip next 2 tr, dc in last tr: 88 dc and 43 ch-3 sps.

Row 3: Ch 4 (**counts as first dc plus ch 1**), turn; (3 dc in next ch-3 sp, ch 1) across to last 2 dc, skip next dc, dc in last dc: 131 dc and 44 ch-1 sps.

Row 4: Ch 3, turn; 2 dc in next ch-1 sp, ch 1, (3 dc in next ch-1 sp, ch 1) across to last ch-1 sp, dc in last ch-1 sp and in last dc: 131 dc and 43 ch-1 sps.

Row 5: Ch 3, turn; dc in next dc, (dc in next ch-1 sp and in next 3 dc) across; finish off: 174 dc.

Row 6: With **right** side facing, join Red with slip st in first dc; ch 4 (**counts as first tr**), tr in next dc changing to White, tr in next 2 dc changing to Red in last tr made, ★ tr in next 2 dc changing to White in last tr made, tr in next 2 dc changing to Red in last tr made; repeat from ★ across to last 2 dc, tr in last 2 dc; finish off Red and cut White.

CENTER STRIP
Working across right edge of Center Strip, work Rows 1-5 of First Strip.
Working across left edge of Center Strip, work Rows 1-6 of First Strip.

LAST STRIP
Working across right edge of Last Strip, work Rows 1-5 of First Strip.

Using Placement Diagram as a guide and Green, whipstitch Strips together.

TRIM

With **right** side facing, join Red with slip st in center dc of first top corner 5-dc group; ch 4, tr in same st changing to White, ♥ tr in same st, tr in next dc changing to Red, tr in next 2 dc changing to White in last tr made, [tr in next 2 dc changing to Red in last tr made, tr in next 2 dc changing to White in last tr made] 6 times; ★ working in end of rows across Borders, [2 tr changing to Red in last tr made, 2 tr changing to White in last tr made] 6 times evenly spaced across, tr in same row as last tr made, tr in next dc changing to Red, tr in next 2 dc changing to White in last tr made, [tr in next 2 dc changing to Red in last tr made, tr in next 2 dc changing to White in last tr made] 6 times; repeat from ★ once **more**, 2 tr in next corner dc changing to Red in last tr made, tr in same corner st; working in each dc and in each joining dc across, tr in next dc changing to White, tr in next 2 dc changing to Red in last tr made, [tr in next 2 dc changing to White in last tr made, tr in next 2 dc changing to Red in last tr made] across to within one dc of center dc of next corner 5-dc group, skip one dc ♥, 2 tr in next corner dc changing to White in last tr made, repeat from ♥ to ♥ once, cut White; join with slip st to first tr, finish off.

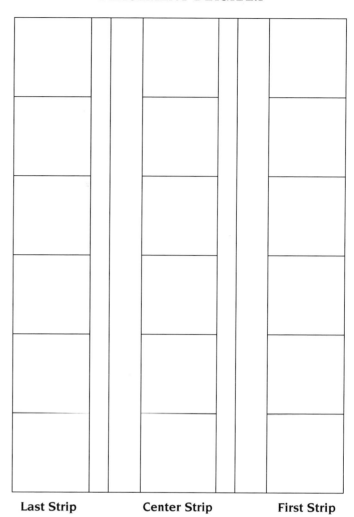

Last Strip   **Center Strip**   **First Strip**

General Instructions

ABBREVIATIONS

BP	Back Post
ch(s)	chain(s)
cm	centimeters
dc	double crochet(s)
dtr	double treble crochet(s)
FPsc	Front Post single crochet(s)
hdc	half double crochet(s)
mm	millimeters
Rnd(s)	Round(s)
sc	single crochet(s)
sp(s)	space(s)
st(s)	stitch(es)
tr	treble crochet(s)
YO	yarn over

★ — work instructions following ★ as many **more** times as indicated in addition to the first time.

† to † or ♥ to ♥ — work all instructions from first † to second † or first ♥ to second ♥ as many times as specified.

( ) or [ ] — work enclosed instructions **as many** times as specified by the number immediately following **or** work all enclosed instructions in the stitch or space indicated **or** contains explanatory remarks.

colon (:) — the number(s) given after a colon at the end of a row or round denote(s) the number of stitches you should have on that row or round.

JOINING WITH SC

When instructed to join with sc, begin with a slip knot on hook. Insert hook in stitch or space indicated, YO and pull up a loop, YO and draw through both loops on hook.

JOINING WITH DC

When instructed to join with dc, begin with a slip knot on hook. YO, holding loop on hook, insert hook in stitch or space indicated, YO and pull up a loop (3 loops on hook), (YO and draw through 2 loops on hook) twice.

GAUGE

Exact gauge is **essential** for proper size. Before beginning your project, make the sample swatch given in the individual instructions in the yarn and hook specified. After completing the swatch, measure it, counting your stitches and rows or rounds carefully. If your swatch is larger or smaller than specified, **make another, changing hook size to get the correct gauge.**

Yarn Weight Symbol & Names	LACE 0	SUPER FINE 1	FINE 2	LIGHT 3	MEDIUM 4	BULKY 5	SUPER BULKY 6
Type of Yarns in Category	Fingering, 10-count crochet thread	Sock, Fingering Baby	Sport, Baby	DK, Light Worsted	Worsted, Afghan, Aran	Chunky, Craft, Rug	Bulky, Roving
Crochet Gauge* Ranges in Single Crochet to 4" (10 cm)	32-42 double crochets**	21-32 sts	16-20 sts	12-17 sts	11-14 sts	8-11 sts	5-9 sts
Advised Hook Size Range	Steel*** 6,7,8 Regular hook B-1	B-1 to E-4	E-4 to 7	7 to I-9	I-9 to K-10.5	K-10.5 to M-13	M-13 and larger

*GUIDELINES ONLY: The chart above reflects the most commonly used gauges and hook sizes for specific yarn categories.

** Lace weight yarns are usually crocheted on larger-size hooks to create lacy openwork patterns. Accordingly, a gauge range is difficult to determine. Always follow the gauge stated in your pattern.

*** Steel crochet hooks are sized differently from regular hooks—the higher the number the smaller the hook, which is the reverse of regular hook sizing.

FREE LOOPS OF A CHAIN

When instructed to work in free loops of a chain, work in loop indicated by arrow (**Fig. 1**).

Fig. 1

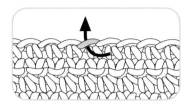

CHANGING COLORS

Work the last stitch to within one step of completion, hook new yarn (**Fig. 2a** or **Fig. 2b**) and draw through all loops on hook. Work over unused yarn when instructed (**Fig. 2c**).

Fig. 2a

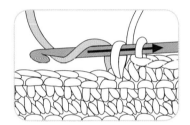

Fig. 2b

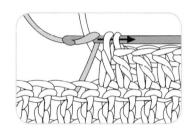

Fig. 2c

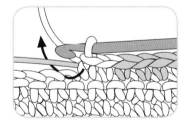

POST STITCH

Work around post of stitch indicated, inserting hook in direction of arrow (**Fig. 3**).

Fig. 3

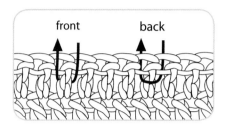

WORKING IN A SPACE BEFORE A STITCH

When instructed to work in space **before** a stitch or in spaces **between** stitches, insert hook in space indicated by arrow (**Fig. 4**).

Fig. 4

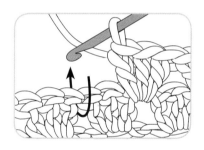

CROCHET TERMINOLOGY		
UNITED STATES		INTERNATIONAL
slip stitch (slip st)	=	single crochet (sc)
single crochet (sc)	=	double crochet (dc)
half double crochet (hdc)	=	half treble crochet (htr)
double crochet (dc)	=	treble crochet(tr)
treble crochet (tr)	=	double treble crochet (dtr)
double treble crochet (dtr)	=	triple treble crochet (ttr)
triple treble crochet (tr tr)	=	quadruple treble crochet (qtr)
skip	=	miss

CROCHET HOOKS												
U.S.	B-1	C-2	D-3	E-4	F-5	G-6	H-8	I-9	J-10	K-10½	N	P	Q
Metric - mm	2.25	2.75	3.25	3.5	3.75	4	5	5.5	6	6.5	9	10	15

WHIPSTITCH

Place two Squares or Panels with **wrong** sides together. Sew through both pieces once to secure the beginning of the seam, leaving an ample yarn end to weave in later. Insert the needle from **front** to **back** through **both** loops on **both** pieces **or** through **inside** loops only of each stitch on **both** pieces (**Fig.** 5*a* **or** *b*). Bring the needle around and insert it from **front** to **back** through next loops of both pieces. Continue in this manner across to next corner, keeping the sewing yarn fairly loose.

Fig. 5a

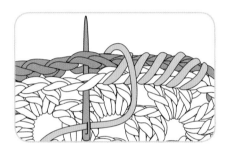

Fig. 5b

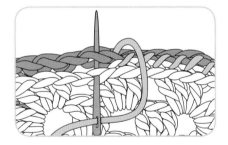

FRINGE

Cut a piece of cardboard 5" (12.5 cm) wide and half as long as specified in individual instructions for strands. Wind the yarn **loosely** and **evenly** around the cardboard lengthwise until the card is filled, then cut across one end; repeat as needed. Hold together as many strands of yarn as specified for the finished fringe, fold in half. With **wrong** side facing and using a crochet hook, draw the folded end up through a row and pull the loose ends through the folded end (**Fig.** 6*a*); draw the knot up **tightly** (**Fig.** 6*b*). Repeat, spacing as desired.
Lay flat on a hard surface and trim the ends.

Fig. 6a

Fig. 6b

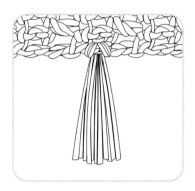

◧□□□ **BEGINNER**	Projects for first-time crocheters using basic stitches. Minimal shaping.
◧■□□ **EASY**	Projects using yarn with basic stitches, repetitive stitch patterns, simple color changes, and simple shaping and finishing.
◧■■□ **INTERMEDIATE**	Projects using a variety of techniques, such as basic lace patterns or color patterns, mid-level shaping and finishing.
◧■■■ **EXPERIENCED**	Projects with intricate stitch patterns, techniques and dimension, such as non-repeating patterns, multi-color techniques, fine threads, small hooks, detailed shaping and refined finishing.

Yarn Information

Each Baby Afghan in this leaflet was made with Light Weight or Medium Weight Yarn. Any brand of Light Weight or Medium Weight Yarn may be used. It is best to refer to the yardage/meters when determining how many balls or skeins to purchase. Remember, to arrive at the finished size, it is the GAUGE/TENSION that is important, not the brand of yarn.

For your convenience, listed below are colors used to create our photography models.

JANUARY
Red Heart® Super Saver®
White - #311 White
Variegated - #345 Baby Print

FEBRUARY
Bernat® Baby Coordinates
Pink - #09412 Sweet Pink
White - #01000 White

MARCH
Red Heart® Super Saver®
Off-White - #313 Aran
Yellow - #322 Pale Yellow
Red Heart® Classic®
Lt Green - #683 Lt Seafoam

APRIL
Premier™ Yarns Everyday Solid
#05 Baby Blue

MAY
Patons® Beehive Baby Sport
White - #09005 Angel White
Yellow - #09615 Sweet Yellow
Lavender - #09317 Little Lavender

JUNE
Lion Brand® Vanna's Choice®
Blue - #107 Sapphire
Orange - #134 Terracotta
Lion Brand® Vanna's Choice® Baby
Yellow - #157 Duckie

JULY
Bernat® Satin Sport
White - #03005 White
Red - #03705 Rouge
Blue - #03110 Marina

AUGUST
Caron® Simply Soft®
White - #9701 White
Green - #9739 Soft Green
Purple - #9717 Orchid

SEPTEMBER
Red Heart® Designer Sport™
Off-White - #3101 Ivory
Brown - #3369 Cocoa
Lion Brand® Baby Soft®
Yellow - #159 Lemon Drop

OCTOBER
Lion Brand® Vanna's Choice®
Variegated - #306 Tangerine Mist
Rust - #135 Rust

NOVEMBER
Red Heart® Designer Sport™
Off-White - #3101 Ivory
Red - #3921 Crimson
Coral - #3261 Terra Cotta

DECEMBER
Red Heart® Sport
Green - #689 Hunter Green
Red - #912 Cherry Red
White - #1 White

We have made every effort to ensure that these instructions are accurate and complete. We cannot, however, be responsible for human error, typographical mistakes, or variations in individual work.

Production Team: Writer/Technical Editor - Lois J. Long; Editorial Writer - Susan McManus Johnson; Senior Graphic Artist - Lora Puls; Graphic Artists - Jacob Casleton and Becca Snider; Photo Stylist - Sandra Daniel; and Photographer - Ken West.

Instructions tested and photo models made by Janet Akins and Marianna Crowder.